Delicious Detox Drinks
How to Make 101 Fruit-Infused Waters

HAILEY MURRAY

Baldwin & Black
18653 Ventura Bvld, #311
Tarzana, California 91356

ISBN: 978-1-942382-01-0

www.baldwinandblack.com

CONTENTS

INTRODUCTION

I have a confession to make. My name is Hailey, and I am a sodaholic. I've been clean and sober now for nine months, but I still hear the sound of someone pulling a Coca-Cola tab and think *I want that. I really want that. I deserve it! Just this once...*

As far as vices go, I know my desperation for soda bears no comparison to the habit of a heroin junkie or meth user. Still, for months and months after quitting I thought about soda all the time; a meal didn't quite feel complete without my trusty liquid sugar sitting next to my plate.

The tragedy was, like many addicts, I *knew* soda was bad for me. I hated the HFCS (High Fructose Corn Syrup) that most soda manufacturers today use in place of real sugar. I loved the first few gulps of frosty cold soda on a sunny day, but hated the metallic aftertaste that reminded me I was drinking something made in a factory, not grown on a farm. I couldn't stand the fuzzy feeling on my teeth, or buying stronger and stronger whitening toothpastes to get rid of the acid yellowing. I hated getting through a day and realizing I'd had more soda to drink than water.

Obviously, something had to change.

I should mention that, unlike many people, I have never had a problem drinking plain water. I love plain water! Few things are as refreshing and easy to gulp as a big, full glass of plain water. Of course, I think infusions can make water taste 10x better, but I don't mind drinking my water straight-up at all.

My problem was that I'd forget to drink that water. Unless I kept a two-quart bottle of water next to the computer in my office (where I write my books, like this one!) I'd simply never reach for water. It wouldn't even cross my mind. I can't tell you how many times I reached the end of the day, realized I'd had practically zero water to drink, and tried to down a one-quart bottle in a minute or two just before bedtime. It wasn't much fun, and neither was waking in the middle of the night when my bladder chose to remind me how much water I'd guzzled right before putting my head down to sleep.

I tried and failed to drink more water for the longest time. I love sparkling water, but that was too expensive for my everyday budget. So were the imported flavored waters from our local 'fancy' food store.

I needed a new way to drink water. I wanted it to taste pure and refreshing, but with no artificial flavors, colorings or preservatives. I wanted convenience, something that would take less than five minutes to put together and only a moment to pour from a jug in the fridge. Ideally, I wanted the 'healthiness' of my experiment with infused waters to go beyond merely staying well-hydrated, and find a way to extract some of the goodness of fruits and herbs into delicious, naturally flavored water.

I thought about the water they serve at my local spa, where my lovely husband has occasionally treated me to a massage or facial treatment. They have a huge cooler of ice-cold water that's always filled with cucumber and lemon slices; it's delicious. I could easily make that! And I could try other things besides lemon and cucumber, like pineapple, or my son's beloved blueberries…

I had my bright idea, but I had no idea what I was getting into. After almost a year preparing, tasting and making notes on countless different infusions, I've compiled my favorite 101 recipes—using *40 types of fruits and herbs*—in this book for you to enjoy.

Now I have a new addiction—infused water. And with so many varieties to try (and so many compliments about my apparently glowing skin!) I'm not giving it up anytime soon.

Forget soda. Drink to your health!

THE BENEFITS OF WATER

While researching this book, I found a truly chilling set of facts: according to a 2013 study by the Centers for Disease Control and Prevention (CDC), *forty-three percent of adults in the US drink less than four cups of water per day.* Even more alarmingly, seven percent drink no water at all. Keep in mind that, while the CDC officially says your daily water needs are determined by your individual body makeup, eight glasses per day is almost universally the recommended place to start.

We live in a nation where (for now, at least) clean, drinkable water is abundant. Most of us don't need to trek a mile with a bucket on our head to collect water from a dirty well; we simply turn on a tap or unscrew a bottle. Water is easy to find, it's cheap, yet for some crazy reason, we're still not drinking enough of it.

Most of us remember the statistic from science class in early schooling: human beings are made up of 60-70% water. This water plays a vital role in our body's digestive system, food absorption, circulation, creation of saliva, nutrient transportation around the body, and maintenance of body temperature.

We gain water by drinking and eating, and lose water through sweating and urination. When you don't drink enough water, your body first tries some ingenious methods to pull fluid away from various parts of itself. By the time you start thinking *I'm thirsty,* you've likely actually needed water—and been operating at less than peak performance—for quite some time.

When we regularly take in less water than we expel, we experience any number of health problems, many of them quite serious. Lost water must be replaced to keep our bodies healthy and functioning. Improper water balance in the body can lead to dry skin, dizziness, headache, fatigue, digestive difficulties, and more.

The good news? Simply drinking more water can benefit our health in a myriad of ways. I've listed some of the major benefits below:

Weight Loss

If you replace a can of soda, juice or smoothie with a zero-calorie serving of water, you've saved anywhere from 120-600 calories. You won't feel deprived, either; some of the sweeter recipes in this book are fine replacements for the 'terrible trio' of sugary drinks.

Drinking a large glass of infused water before a meal will fill you up and help you exercise portion control; numerous studies have shown that dieters eat less and lose more weight when they drink enough water to feel a little full before a meal.

Energized Muscles

Cells without the proper balance of fluids and electrolytes shrivel, resulting in muscle fatigue. Dehydrated muscles simply don't perform well. The American College of Sports Medicine recommends that people drink about 17 ounces (a tiny bit more than two cups) about two hours before exercise. They also recommend stopping frequently to drink some more during your workout.

Beautiful Skin

Let's stop talking about health for a moment and be a little vain: a well-hydrated face is a beautiful face. Hydrating from the inside makes skin much more luminous. If you'd like to have soft, glowing and clean skin that minimizes the look of any fine lines and wrinkles, your best prescription is not a $200 face cream; it's drinking a lot more water. (Why didn't they tell you that at the cosmetics counter? Because it's their job to sell $200 face cream, not water.)

Another thing they won't tell you at the cosmetics counter is that there's no way to cure cellulite. No lotion, potion, drug or spa treatment can get rid of those pesky dimples completely—but hydrated, 'pumped up' cells can make the appearance of cellulite and wrinkles less noticeable.

What's more, both dry skin *and* acne can be improved or eliminated by drinking more water.

Flush Out Toxins

The water in your body transports waste products in and out of cells. Body fluids help remove toxins, like the water-soluble blood urea nitrogen, through the kidneys to be excreted in urine.

Have you ever noticed that your urine changes color depending on how many fluids you've had that day? When you're getting enough, your urine should be almost clear and free of odor. If your urine is dark or has an odor (and there's no other explanation—for example, some vitamins will turn your urine bright orange, and eating asparagus can create a strange smell in your urine) you need to drink more water!

If you rarely or never drink enough to keep your body functioning as it should, you're at risk of developing painful kidney stones.

End Constipation

Water also plays an important role in the digestive system. It keeps food flowing through the gastrointestinal tract, and prevents constipation. (When you're not drinking enough water, your body will get those vital fluids from wherever it can—including pulling it from your stool to maintain hydration. That's why failing to drink enough water can cause dry, hard stools and subsequent constipation.)

Boost Your Brain Power

Your brain consists of even more water than the rest of your body—around eighty-five percent. When your brain is functioning on a full reserve of water, you will be able to think faster, be more focused, and experience greater clarity.

A 2013 study from the UK found that even mild dehydration might have a negative effect on the brain's performance. The study participants were tested with a variety of mental challenges on two separate mornings—once after drinking a glass of water and eating a granola bar, and the next time after simply eating the granola bar (study participants were expected to fast overnight before the testing dates).

The researchers concluded that drinking enough water can improve the brain's power to complete tasks that require a speedy response. Remarkably, the test subjects who reported the greatest thirst experienced a bigger mental boost after drinking water than subjects who didn't feel as thirsty.

Improve Circulation

Have you ever experienced painful leg cramps, or back pain that comes and goes? You may be suffering from the effects of drinking too little water. Drinking enough water is vital for fluid-electrolyte balance in the body, and helps to improve blood circulation. Drink more water and you may get rid of those cramps for good.

And Remember...

All these are just a few of the benefits of *plain* water; we're going to be making infused water, with fruits and herbs that have health benefits of their own. At the end of this book, you'll find a comprehensive listing of all forty ingredients featured in my infusions and their unique healing powers. I'm not content to simply get you hydrated; I want you feeling stronger, more energetic, and in better health than ever before.

In the next chapter, we'll learn more about these nutritional powerhouses, and how to make them part of your everyday life.

WHY INFUSE YOUR WATER?

Before we really get started, a few words about me: I'm not a professional chef, and I don't have a line of products on a home shopping network or a stoneware collection available at Target. I'm a suburban working mother, and if I can make one or two infusions each night to drink the next day, I promise you can, too.

There are many benefits to making your own infused water. At the end of this book, you'll find a complete listing of all the ingredients used in the recipes contained here, and the healthful properties they each contain; for now, let's talk about the general benefits of infused water.

- Simple to make; can be prepared in 2-5

minutes

- Excellent source of vitamins, minerals, antioxidants and nutrients
- Zero fat, zero calories, no artificial sweeteners or ingredients
- A tasty, healthy substitute for soda, juice, and sugar-loaded 'vitamin drinks' and 'sports drinks'
- Popular with children; a great way to get kids to switch from sugar-laden juice or soda
- Depending on the infusion, may be energizing, calming, cleansing, rejuvenating or strengthening
- Fruits used for infusion can be reused, e.g. in a smoothie or simply eaten whole
- Can be turned into 'soda' with a carbonation machine

Want more benefits? Take flavor – I've tried the store-brand vitamin waters and energy drinks, and they have nothing on the vibrant taste of a fresh, homemade infused water.

Homemade infused waters both taste better and are infinitely healthier than the chemical-laden drinks you might find at the store. And, unlike store-bought drinks, the tastes you can create with infused waters are limited only by your imagination.

There's another reason to avoid store-bought drinks. Unless you're buying the fanciest—and most expensive—bottled drinks, the label likely won't tell you where the ingredients inside came from. Wouldn't you rather know that the blueberries in your blueberry-infused water come from a local farmer, instead of thousands of miles away in Argentina? Making your own infused waters means *you* are in charge of quality control and know exactly what you and your family are drinking.

Here's another benefit—cost. You can easily make infused water in an empty, thoroughly washed old plastic or glass container (from the last bottle of water you'll ever buy, perhaps) and whatever fruits or herbs you happen to have around the house. If you currently buy just one $3 drink per day, you'll save more than $1000 a year making your own infused water instead.

Flavored waters are also wonderful conversation starters. Next time you serve these colorful, flavorful drinks at a party (especially at an outdoor, summer grill or picnic—perfect for refreshing infused water) expect plenty of compliments on the taste and beautiful look of the drinks you prepared, along with enthusiastic guests begging for your recipes! (I hope you'll steer them towards this book instead. Less work for you, more book sales for me.)

If you're a parent, giving your children a taste of infused water instead of juice or soda is one of the best gifts you can bestow on them. According to the USDA, the average child under 12 consumes an enormous 49lbs of added sugar each year. That's more than twelve teaspoons per day! A huge percentage of that comes from soda and juice, which may seem healthier (it's *usually* made from fruit) but is just as full of sugar as soda. Let's not even get me started on chocolate milk…

My toddler son adores most of my infused waters; he loves plain water too. I'm proud he's growing up healthy and without taste buds conditioned to expect sweet, sweet and more sweet. Of course, feel free to check back in when he reaches his teens and his high school has a soda machine

INFUSION: THE BASICS

Here's the good news: everything about infusing water is basic. It's one of the simplest things you can prepare in a kitchen. In fact, you don't even need a kitchen!

I've written every recipe in this book to make a little over one quart (approximately one liter, or four cups) of infused water. If, like me, you sometimes find yourself making three, four or even five quarts of the same delicious recipe, simply multiply the quantities in the recipe.

Here's how to make infused water: gather your fruits and herbs, and prepare them as written in the recipe (for example, by peeling or slicing). Place them in a jar or bottle. Add water. Leave in the fridge for four to twenty-four hours.

That's it. I told you it was simple!

If you've placed all your fruits and herbs in your jar or bottle and don't have enough room for the 4 cups of water I suggest for most recipes, don't worry—you'll just end up with more concentrated flavor in your water. You can drink it that way (there's nothing bad about extra flavor) or dilute your infused water with plain water before drinking.

It's a good idea to keep your water covered as it's infusing, so if your container doesn't have a lid, try adding a layer of ice over the top. You can also use aluminum foil or saran wrap.

It's practically impossible to 'screw up' a fruit or herb infusion. If you accidentally dump too much mint into your recipe (it said 1/4 cup, but you put in 4 cups. Oops) or get halfway through making an infusion before realizing you are *completely* out of lemons, a seemingly essential ingredient in the recipe, don't worry. You're not making mistakes. You're creating new flavors!

To write this book, *I* created almost one thousand infusions. Some were obviously better than others, which is why they made it into this book; some were so-so; only a few were flat out undrinkable (this coming from a woman who happily drinks raw collard juice). The best of my recipes are included here, and while I believe this is the most comprehensive book about infused water available today, my recipes are not claiming or intending to be the be-all-and-end-all when it comes to infused water.

So experiment. Get in touch with your taste buds—would this taste better if it were a little more sweet, tart, bitter, or had a little kick of ginger, or even jalapeño? They're *your* taste buds, so only you know will know which mixes seem made for you. Treat my recipes as guideposts along your journey.

I do encourage you to use as many different types of produce as you can; there's an incredible array of fruits, herbs and even vegetables out there for you to discover, and each has a unique taste as well as valuable health-promoting properties. If you live near a farmers' market, count yourself very lucky, and try to scour the place each week hunting for the freshest, most delicious in-season produce.

If you can't find fresh produce, don't give up—frozen fruits can also be used in infusions, and for many months of the year, that's what I use to keep the taste of summer (mmm, raspberries...) alive in my water.

If you're concerned about the costs of fresh fruit, remember you can use the same fruits for infusion for up to twenty-four hours. Simply infuse one batch of water for eight hours or so, drain the infused water and store or drink it, and refill your container with the fruit still inside with more water for another round of infusion. The infused water itself should also be consumed or frozen within 24 hours. You can also top up your water container as you go, adding more water every time you drink a glass.

Finally, if you have access to filtered water, and even better, filtered water *and* glass or BPA-free plastic jars or bottles for infusing, please make good use of them.

The purifying, healthful effects of these infused drinks are weakened when you're swallowing them with chemicals in tap water or with trace amounts of BPA, a common component in many plastic containers known to be dangerous to human health. In my humble opinion, glass bottles and mason jars and BPA-free plastic bottles are worth the small investment to make your infused waters as pure and clean as possible.

Now let's get to the recipes! You'll find a list of each ingredient and its health benefits at the end of this book. You'll also find a detailed index with each recipe listed by ingredient, so you can find your favorites easily.

ONE-INGREDIENT RECIPES

Blackberry
1 cup blackberries
4 cups water

Blueberry
1 cup blueberries
4 cups water

Cucumber
½ cucumber, sliced
4 cups water

Grapefruit
¼ grapefruit, sliced
4 cups water

Lemon
1 lemon, sliced
4 cups water

Lime
1 lime, sliced
4 cups water

Orange
½ orange, sliced
4 cups water

Raspberry
½ cup raspberries
4 cups water

Strawberry
1 cup strawberries, sliced
4 cups water

Vanilla
1 vanilla bean
4 cups water

Watermelon
1 cup watermelon, cubed
4 cups water

TWO-INGREDIENT RECIPES

Apple and Blueberry
½ apple, seeds removed and sliced
½ cup blueberries
4 cups water

Apple and Cinnamon
1 apple, seeds removed and sliced
1 cinnamon stick
4 cups water

Apple and Lime
1 apple, seeds removed and sliced
½ lime, sliced
4 cups water

Basil and Mango
4-5 basil leaves
½ mango, peeled and cubed
4 cups water

Basil and Raspberry
1-2 basil leaves
¼ cup raspberries
4 cups water

Basil and Strawberry
1 large or two small basil leaves
¼ cup strawberries, sliced
4 cups water

Basil and Watermelon
2-3 basil leaves
1 cup watermelon, cubed
4 cups water

Blackberry and Sage
½ cup blackberries
1 sage leaf
4 cups water

Blueberry and Lemon
¼ cup blueberries
¼ lemon, sliced
4 cups water

Cacao and Coconut
2 tbsp cacoa powder
4 cups coconut water

Cantaloupe and Mint
½ cup cantaloupe, cubed
2-3 mint sprigs
4 cups water

Cantaloupe and Watermelon
½ cup cantaloupe, cubed
½ cup watermelon, cubed
4 cups water

Cherry and Vanilla
½ cup cherries, pits removed
1 vanilla bean
4 cups water

Cherry and Pineapple
¼ cup cherries, pits removed
¼ cup pineapple, cubed
4 cups water

Chili and Cucumber
2 chilies, seeds removed, chopped
½ cucumber, sliced
4 cups water

Cranberry and Orange
½ cup cranberries
1 orange, sliced
4 cups water

Cucumber and Lemon
¼ cucumber, sliced
¼ lemon, sliced
4 cups water

Cucumber and Mint
¼ cup cucumber, sliced
2-3 sprigs mint
4 cups water

Ginger and Lemon
2 slices fresh ginger, peeled
½ lemon, sliced
4 cups water

Ginger and Lemongrass

3-4 slices fresh ginger, peeled

1 stalk lemongrass

4 cups water

Ginger and Peach

1-2 slices fresh ginger, peeled

1 peach, pit removed, cubed

4 cups water

Grape and Grapefruit

½ cup seedless grapes, halved

¼ grapefruit, sliced

4 cups water

Grapefruit and Lime

¼ grapefruit, sliced

¼ lime, sliced

4 cups water

Grapefruit and Orange

1 grapefruit, sliced

1 orange, sliced

4 cups water

Honeydew and Lime
1 honeydew slice, rind removed and cubed
½ lime, sliced
4 cups water

Watermelon and Jalapeño
1/3 jalapeño pepper, seeds and stem removed
½ cup watermelon, cubed
4 cups water

Kiwi and Mango
2 kiwi fruits, peeled and sliced
1 mango, pitted, peeled and cubed
4 cups water

Kiwi and Strawberry
2 kiwi fruits, sliced
4 strawberries, sliced
4 cups water

Lavender and Lemon
1 ½ lemons, sliced
3-4 fresh lavender sprigs
4 cups water

Lavender and Mint
1 sprig fresh lavender
2 sprigs fresh mint
4 cups water

Lemon and Lime
¼ lemon, sliced
¼ lime, sliced
4 cups water

Lemon and Orange
¼ lemon, sliced
½ orange, sliced
4 cups water

Lemon and Plum
½ lemon, sliced
2 plums, pits removed
4 cups water

Lemon and Pomegranate
¼ lemon, sliced
½ cup pomegranate seeds
4 cups water

Lemon and Strawberry
¼ lemon, sliced
½ cup strawberries, sliced
4 cups water

Lime and Papaya
1 lime, sliced
1 papaya, peeled and cubed
4 cups water

Lime and Raspberry
¼ lime, sliced
¼ cup raspberries
4 cups water

Lime and Strawberry
½ lime, peeled and chopped
½ cup strawberries, sliced
4 cups water

Mango and Orange
½ mango, pitted, peeled, and cubed
½ orange, sliced

Mango and Pineapple
½ cup mango, cubed
½ cup pineapple, cubed
4 cups water

Mint and Orange
1 sprig fresh mint
½ orange, sliced
4 cups water

Mint and Pineapple
4 sprigs fresh mint
¾ cup pineapple, cubed
4 cups water

Mint and Watermelon
2 sprigs fresh mint
1 cup watermelon, cubed
4 cups water

Mixed Berries and Rosemary
1 cup mixed berries
1 large sprig fresh rosemary
4 cups water

Pear and Raspberry
1 pear, seeds removed and sliced
1 sprig fresh rosemary

Pineapple and Raspberry
¼ cup pineapple, cubed
¼ cup raspberries
four cups water

Pomegranate and Raspberry
½ cup pomegranate seeds
½ cup raspberries
4 cups water

Rosemary and Watermelon
1 sprig fresh rosemary
½ cup watermelon, cubed
4 cups water

Strawberry and Vanilla
½ cup strawberries, sliced
1 vanilla bean
4 cups water

THREE-INGREDIENT RECIPES

Apple, Blueberry and Mint
¼ apple, seeds removed and sliced
½ cup blueberries
2-3 mint sprigs
4 cups water

Apple, Blueberry and Plum
1 apple, seeds removed and sliced
½ cup blueberries
1 plum, pit removed
4 cups water

Apple, Cinnamon and Ginger
1 apple, seeds removed and sliced
1 cinnamon stick
1-2 fresh slices ginger, peeled
4 cups water

Basil, Blueberry and Lemon
1-2 basil leaves
½ cup blueberries
¼ lemon
4 cups water

Basil, Cucumber and Lemon
10 basil leaves
½ cucumber, sliced
½ lemon, sliced
4 cups water

Basil, Lemon and Lime
1 basil leaf
1 lemon, sliced
1 lime, sliced
4 cups water

Basil, Peach and Vanilla
5 basil leaves
1 peach, pit removed and cubed
1 vanilla bean
4 cups water

Blackberry, Ginger and Lemon

1 cup blackberries

2-3 slices fresh ginger, peeled

½ lemon, sliced

4 cups water

Blueberry, Mint and Strawberry

½ cup blueberries

2-3 mint sprigs

½ cup strawberries, sliced

4 cups water

Blueberry, Pineapple and Strawberry

½ cup blueberries

¼ cup pineapple, cubed

¼ cup strawberries, sliced

4 cups water

Blueberry, Strawberry and Vanilla

½ cup blueberries

¼ cup strawberries, sliced

1 vanilla bean

4 cups water

Blueberry, Raspberry and Lemon
½ cup blueberries
½ cup raspberries
1 lemon, sliced
4 cups water

Blueberry, Raspberry and Strawberry
¼ cup blueberries
¼ cup raspberries
¼ cup strawberries, sliced
4 cups water

Cantaloupe, Cucumber and Mint
½ cucumber, sliced
2 slices cantaloupe, cubed
4-5 sprigs fresh mint
4 cups water

Cantaloupe, Honeydew and Watermelon
¼ cup cantaloupe, cubed
¼ cup honeydew, cubed
¼ cup watermelon, cubed
4 cups water

Cherry, Cucumber and Mint

½ cup cherries, pits removed

½ cucumber, sliced

1-2 sprigs fresh mint

4 cups water

Cranberry, Lemon and Mint

½ cup cranberries, cut

½ lemon, sliced

1-2 sprigs fresh mint

4 cups water

Cucumber, Grapefruit and Strawberry

¼ cup cucumber

½ small pink grapefruit, sliced

½ cup strawberries, sliced

4 cups water

Cucumber, Lemon and Lemongrass

½ cucumber, sliced

½ lemon, sliced

1 stalk lemongrass

4 cups water

Cucumber, Lime and Mint
¼ cucumber, sliced
½ lime, sliced
4-5 sprigs fresh mint
4 cups water

Ginger, Lemon and Strawberry
2-3 slices fresh ginger, peeled
½ lemon, sliced
½ cup strawberries
4 cups water

Ginger, Lime and Papaya
2-3 slices fresh ginger, peeled
½ lime, sliced
½ cup papaya, peeled and cubed
4 cups water

Grapefruit, Lemon and Orange
¼ grapefruit, sliced
¼ lemon, sliced
¼ orange, sliced
4 cups water

Grapefruit, Rosemary and Sage

¼ grapefruit, sliced

1 sprig rosemary

2-3 sage leaves

4 cups water

Green Tea, Raspberry and Strawberry

4 bags green tea (keep leaves inside tea bags)

½ cup raspberries

½ cup strawberries

4 cups water

Kiwi, Lemon and Pineapple

½ kiwi fruit, sliced

¼ lemon, sliced

½ cup pineapple, cubed

4 cups water

Lemon, Mint and Strawberry

¼ lemon, sliced

2-3 sprigs fresh mint

½ cup strawberries, sliced

4 cups water

Lime, Mint and Raspberry

1 lime, sliced

4 sprigs fresh mint

1 lime, sliced

4 cups water

Orange, Pineapple and Strawberry

¼ orange, sliced

½ cup strawberries, sliced

½ cup pineapple, cubed

4 cups water

FOUR-INGREDIENT RECIPES

Blackberry, Blueberry, Lemon and Raspberry
2 tbsp blackberries
2 tbsp blueberries
¼ lemon, sliced
2 tbsp raspberries
4 cups water

Blackberry, Blueberry, Mint and Raspberry
¼ cup blackberries
¼ cup blueberries
2-3 sprigs fresh mint
¼ cup raspberries
4 cups water

Blueberry, Lemon, Mint and Peach
¼ cup blueberries
¼ lemon, sliced
1 mint leaf
½ peach, cubed
4 cups water

Blueberry, Lemon, Raspberry and Strawberry
¼ cup blueberries
¼ lemon, sliced
¼ cup raspberries
¼ cup strawberries, sliced
4 cups water

Blueberry, Raspberry, Rosemary and Vanilla
¼ cup blueberries
¼ cup raspberries
1 large sprig rosemary
1 vanilla bean
4 cups water

Cilantro, Lemon, Lime and Orange
2 tbsp cilantro leaves
½ lemon, sliced
½ lime, sliced
½ orange, sliced
4 cups water

Cinnamon, Ginger, Pear and Vanilla

1 cinnamon stick
2-3 slices fresh ginger, peeled
½ pear, seeds removed and sliced
1 vanilla bean
4 cups water

Cucumber, Grapefruit, Lemon and Lime

½ cucumber, sliced
½ grapefruit, sliced
½ lemon, sliced
½ lime, sliced
4 cups water

Ginger, Mint, Orange and Pineapple

1-2 slices fresh ginger, peeled
2-3 sprigs fresh mint
½ orange, sliced
½ cup pineapple, cubed
4 cups water

THE ESSENTIAL INGREDIENTS

Did you know that blueberries may improve your memory, or that apples can fight off allergies? You probably already know that cranberries can help fight off a urinary tract infection, but did you know that the very same compound also helps to prevent tooth decay?

There are 40 delicious fruits and herbs used in the recipes in this book, and listing all the marvelous benefits of each one would take a lifetime! I've compiled only the most important benefits here, to inspire you to include a fruit or herb you wouldn't normally use in your next infused water.

Please note that I am not a medical doctor or trained nutritionist or herbalist; while I have gathered this information from the most reliable sources I could find, you should *always* plan a visit with your doctor before changing your diet or eating habits.

 **Apples**

Apples contain flavonoids, antioxidants which may help lower the chance of developing diabetes and asthma. They're also a natural breath freshener. Don't peel your apples while preparing to infuse them; most of the nutrients and flavor are found in and just below the skin, including quercetin, an antioxidant with antihistamine (anti-allergy) and anti-inflammatory powers.

 **Basil**

Basil contains both antioxidant flavonoids

and anti-inflammatory, anti-bacterial natural oils. These anti-inflammatory properties may provide symptomatic relief from rheumatoid arthritis and inflammatory bowel syndrome.

 Blackberries

The deep purple color of blackberries comes from the powerful antioxidant anthocyanin, which may reduce the risk of cancer and stroke. Scientists are also investigating whether blackberry extract may be able to stop the growth of existing cancers.

 **Blueberries**

Blueberries are extremely rich in antioxidants, and may dramatically help your brain function as you age. Several studies link blueberry consumption with a better memory, and blueberries have been linked to a lower risk of Parkinson's and Alzheimer's diseases. They are also rich in manganese, which boosts your metabolism and can help you stay slim.

 Cacao

Cacao is rich in beneficial antioxidants; in fact, one study showed that it contained more antioxidants than black tea, green tea or red wine. The particular antioxidants found in cacao can prevent LDL (the 'bad' cholesterol) from hardening and forming plaque in your arteries, improving circulation and reducing the risk of heart disease.

 **Cantaloupes**

Cantaloupe is your secret weapon for smoother, younger-looking skin, thanks to its high content of vitamin A, which boosts cell reproduction. Rich in the antioxidant beta-carotene, cantaloupe may also help prevent the development of cataracts.

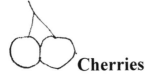 **Cherries**

Cherries are rich in vitamin C; they also contain more of the antioxidant anthocyanin than any other fruit. This potent antioxidant may help reduce inflammation in the body and ease the pain of gout and arthritis.

 **Chilies**

The spicy flavor in chilies comes from a compound called capsaicin, which has anti-bacterial and pain-relieving qualities, and may also prevent the development of certain cancers and diabetes. It may also reduce 'bad' LDL cholesterol levels.

Cilantro

Cilantro contains valuable antioxidant and anti-bacterial compounds; it is also being studied as a natural water purifier, after preliminary research showed it could prevent lead build-up in animals.

Cinnamon

Cinnamon is a true superfood; I'd need to write another book to list all its amazing properties! Cinnamon assists in regulating blood sugar, especially for those with diabetes; it has been used to treat medication-resistant yeast infections; it may relieve the systems of irritable bowel syndrome and acute 'stomach bugs', and it's also a powerful memory booster.

Did I mention it can even combat PMS?

Coconut Water

Dubbed 'nature's sports drink', coconut water is full of electrolytes that can stabilize the fluid balance in the body and rapidly rehydrate you after athletic activity. It's also the only ingredient in this book that will add calories to an infusion; expect an eight-ounce serving to include about forty calories

Cranberries

With their strong antibacterial properties, cranberries are known for easing urinary tract infections. They have also been linked to the prevention of kidney stones and ulcers. Drinking cranberry-infused water may benefit your teeth, too; those same antibacterial powers fight the bacteria that cause cavities.

Cucumber

Cucumbers contain a powerful anti-inflammatory compound called fisetin that may play a vital role in brain health. In addition to improving memory and protecting nerve cells from age-related damage, early research has suggested it could prevent memory and learning impairment in patients with Alzheimer's disease.

Ginger

Ginger is a powerful weapon against gastrointestinal distress; it's long been known for its stomach-calming properties in people suffering from indigestion, and is also often prescribed as a safe, natural remedy for morning sickness and nausea in pregnant women. It also contains anti-inflammatory compounds called gingerols that can provide symptomatic relief to those suffering from arthritis.

Grapes

Grapes contain resveratrol, an antioxidant that may reduce blood pressure, lower the risk of blood clots, and help to prevent heart disease. Promising new research suggests resveratrol may also help to stop the spread of breast, stomach and colon cancers.

Grapefruits

Grapefruits may help prevent heart disease by lowering cholesterol. Like other citrus fruits, it is also high in vitamin C, a potent antioxidant which is required for collagen synthesis in the body. Collagen is a structural protein required for maintaining strong blood vessels, skin, organs and bones.

Green Tea

With its combination of mild caffeine and the amino acid L-theanine, green tea is rightly known as a brain booster; it may aid in cognition and reduce anxiety. Green tea has also been shown to increase your metabolism and aid in weight loss, and it also has powerful antioxidant effects.

Honeydew Melons

Honeydew melons are high in vitamin C, a powerful antioxidant. They also contain a good amount of potassium, a mineral and electrolyte that is essential for nerve and muscle function.

Jalapeños

Like other chilies, jalapenos are rich in vitamin C and capsaicin, an anti-inflammatory compound that promotes healthy blood flow. Capsaicin has also shown promise for weight loss, by speeding up the metabolism.

Kiwi Fruit

Kiwi fruits actually contain more vitamin C than oranges, and help to maintain strong bones, cartilage, teeth and gums. They can also lower the level of triglycerides in your blood, potentially lowering your risk of heart disease.

Lavender

Research has shown that lavender may be useful for treating anxiety, insomnia, depression, digestive issues, nausea, and abdominal bloating. Lavender can also be used to relieve pain from headaches, sprains and sores.

Lemons

Lemon has been used as an effective treatment for sore throats, indigestion, constipation, some respiratory disorders, and high blood pressure. It is also believed to improve the beauty of the hair and skin, and is a very common ingredient in 'detox' preparations.

Lemongrass

Anti-inflammatory, anti-bacterial and anti-fungal, lemongrass is truly a miracle ingredient. It is high in iron, making it helpful for people with anemia. It is also said to aid in purifying the body and kick-starting weight loss.

 Limes

Limes are high in vitamin C, which boosts your body's immune response. They also contain the compound kaempferol, which has been shown to stop cancer growth in several studies.

 Mangoes

Mangoes are a rich source of iron, and are

especially helpful for people with anemia or post-menopausal women. Mangoes are also high in the antioxidants zeaxanthin and lutein, which may help protect vision and prevent age-related macular degeneration and subsequent blindness.

 Mint

Mint contains an antioxidant called rosmarinic acid, a natural antihistamine that may relieve seasonal allergies. Mint also contains menthol, a decongestant that helps to break up mucus and alleviate cold and flu systems. It may also ease symptoms of irritable bowel syndrome.

 Oranges

Everyone knows oranges are rich in

immune-boosting vitamin C; not as many people know they also contain collagen, beneficial for maintaining younger-looking skin. They also contain hesperidin, a photochemical which may lower blood triglyceride and cholesterol levels. I advise against peeling oranges before placing them in your infusions; half the vitamin C of oranges is in the pith beneath the skin, and orange peel helps to eliminate bad breath and prevent tooth decay.

Papayas

Papayas contain papain, an enzyme that assists with digestion. They are also high in vitamins A and E, which may help protect against heart disease and colon cancer.

Peaches

Peaches are high in vitamin A, and may help to regulate the immune system and fight off infections.

Pears

Pears contain compounds known to help with type II diabetes; they also may help relieve inflammation and prevent heart disease. Like apples, I suggest you keep the skins on; most of the beneficial ingredients are found in the pear's colorful skin.

Pineapple

Pineapple contains enzymes that improve your skin's elasticity and softness. One of these enzymes, bromelian, helps aid digestion and may also help prevent blood clots, slow the growth of cancer cells, and speed wound healing.

Pink Grapefruits

Pink grapefruits contain lycopene and flavonoids, which may guard against certain types of cancer. The pectin in grapefruit may also help to lower cholesterol.

Plums

A fruit that fights anxiety? Plums contain an antioxidant called chlorogenic acid, which has been linked to a decrease in anxiety-related behaviors.

Pomegranates

Pomegranates contain antioxidant tannins, which are important for heart health. A compound in pomegranates called punicalagin has been shown to lower blood pressure and cholesterol levels. Consuming pomegranates can also prevent plaque from building up in your arteries, causing atherosclerosis.

Raspberries

Raspberries are rich in an antioxidant named ellagic acid, which may help prevent cervical cancer. Studies suggest raspberries may also help treat cancer in the esophagus and colon.

Rosemary

Rosemary is a 'brain herb'; it's known for improving memory and concentration, protecting against neurological damage, and preventing brain aging. It is also rich in antioxidants and may be helpful in treating indigestion.

Sage

Another powerful 'brain herb', sage may improve memory and brain function, and improve memory and decrease feelings of agitation in Alzheimer's patients. It also shows promise in the treatment of type II diabetes.

Strawberries

Strawberries are rich in anti-inflammatory antioxidants, and may help prevent atherosclerosis and suppress the progression of cancer. They also contain folic acid, which is especially important for women planning a pregnancy.

Vanilla

Vanilla contains an antioxidant called vanillin, which acts to decrease inflammation in the body. Other health benefits of vanilla include its ability to act as a mild sedative for sleep and its function as an antidepressant.

Watermelon

Watermelons are rich in lycopene, which can help to prevent heart disease, diabetes, age-related macular degeneration and cataracts, and osteoporosis. It also helps your skin look younger, and has one pretty amazing superpower—it acts as an internal sunscreen, and regular lycopene consumption can actually help to protect your skin from sunburn.

RECIPES BY INGREDIENT

Apple

Basil

Cacao

Cantaloupe

Cranberry

Cucumber

Ginger

Grape

Grapefruit

Green Tea

Green Tea, Raspberry and Strawberry 48

Honeydew

Canteloupe, Honeydew and Watermelon ... 45

Honeydew and Lime 37

Jalapeño

Jalapeño and Watermelon 37

Kiwi Fruit

Kiwi, Lemon and Pineapple ....….... 48

Kiwi and Mango 37

Kiwi and Strawberry 37

Lavender

Lavender and Lemon 37

Lavender and Mint ....…... 38

Lemon

Basil, Blueberry and Lemon ....

Lemongrass

Lime

Mango

Mint

Mixed Berries

Orange

Papaya

Peach

Pear

Pineapple

Plum

Pomegranate

Raspberry

Rosemary

Sage

Strawberry

ABOUT THE AUTHOR

Hailey Murray is the Senior Publisher for Baldwin and Black, a Los Angeles-based publishing house. In her spare time she likes to write, practice krav maga (a no-holds-barred martial art), and cook for her family.

Printed in Great Britain
by Amazon